Rose Kuntz Book & DVD.
The Utterly Amazing
World of Dyslexia.
"Mommy, why is it so hard for me to read?"

DATE DUE			

"Mommy, why is it so hard for me to read?"

The Utterly Amazing World of Dyslexia

Rose Kuntz

"Mommy, why is it so hard for me to read?"

The Utterly Amazing World of Dyslexia

ROSE KUNTZ

www.dyslexiathinktank.org

Copyright © 2010 by Rose Kuntz

ISBN 978-0-578-05084-3

Illustrations by Julia Berman
Layout by Val Sherer, Personalized Publishing Services
Cover design by Kristi Frlekin

Printed in the USA

This book and my work with
The Dyslexia Think Tank
are inspired by two brilliant dyslexics:
my late brother, Harold Grilliot,
and my son, Chris.
Through them my mind has been opened
to the incredible world of dyslexia.

Mommy, why is it so hard for me to read? Why can't I read like the other kids?

You have dyslexia. This means you use the right side of your brain more than the left side. The good readers in your class use the left side of their brains. Dyslexia makes it harder for you to read than the other kids because of this. Having dyslexia means that you are very creative and gifted.

How did I get to be this way?

You were born primarily right brained just like many other very smart people. In fact, many of the world's most brilliant scientists, leaders, writers, musicians and artists all had dyslexia. Let me tell you about a few of these great people.

Albert Einstein did not speak until age four and did not learn to read until he was nine years old. He was a slow student who kept to himself and daydreamed much of the day. When he sat in a classroom, he had a lot of difficulty understanding what the teacher was saying. When he was young like you, he dreamed about becoming a great physicist. Now years later, many people consider him to be the most brilliant person who has ever lived.

Wow, he sounds a lot like me. I sometimes have a hard time understanding my teacher.

Thomas Edison was thrown out of school at age 12. His teachers thought he was not intelligent enough to be in school. He had a hard time focusing on math, reading and other subjects. Young Thomas dreamed about lighting up his room with a light bulb. As an adult, he invented more things than anyone else who has ever lived. At the time of his death, he held over 100 U.S. patents. His best known inventions are the light bulb and phonograph. The phonograph was the first machine that allowed recorded music to be played back. It led to the CD player and I-pod. Imagine what life would be like without lights and recorded music.

Edison must have felt he was not too smart also. But he had to be pretty smart to invent all those things.

That's right.

Agatha Christie had very poor handwriting and her spelling was atrocious. Agatha dreamed about characters and stories that she could write about. She would dictate her words to someone else who wrote them down. She would then have someone else check her writings for language errors. Agatha is best known for her characters of Hercule Poirot and Miss Marple. Her books have sold over a billion copies in the English language and another billion in other languages. Agatha is the most famous mystery writer in the world. Imagine that.

Wow, I have seen Miss Marple on T.V.

George Washington had problems with reading and language. Young George dreamed about being a great leader. As an adult, he first became the Commander in Chief of the Continental Army. After he led his army to defeat the British, George then helped to write the United States Constitution and was instrumental in creating the new nation of the United States of America. All of that led to his being elected our first President.

Wow, George Washington was a dyslexic also?

Yes.

Alexander Graham Bell is another dyslexic that had to work extra hard at school. He dreamed about being able to talk to people in other places without going there. When he grew up he invented the telephone. Imagine what our life would be without telephones. Bell also worked on creating machines that fly and boats that float above the water called hydrofoils.

What would everyone do without their cell phones?

Next I will tell you about Hans Christian Andersen. He struggled with spelling and words. Young Hans dreamed about writing fairy tales. Despite his spelling and strange word formations, he created some incredible stories. You will recognize most of these. He wrote the "Little Mermaid", "The Ugly Ducking", and "The Emperor's New Clothes". The world would be a sadder place without these incredible tales.

I know these stories. They are incredible. He was also a dyslexic?

Yes and there are more.

John Lennon had difficulties with school. He preferred to draw and doodle instead of study. Young John dreamed of becoming a famous musician. Later he helped start a group, the Beatles. He wrote some of the best known songs ever written such as "Strawberry Fields Forever", "Norwegian Wood", "In My Life" and his best known work "Imagine". In "Imagine" he sang about being a dreamer. He definitely was a dreamer who brought great joy and happiness to the world with his music.

So even John Lennon was dyslexic? I know his music. Our teacher plays his songs all the time.

Leonardo da Vinci wrote many of his notes backwards, writing from right to left. Young Leonardo dreamed about becoming an artist. He later painted the Mona Lisa and the Last Supper. Leonardo's paintings and sculptures are displayed all over Italy, France and Europe. Leonardo is one of the best known artists that has ever lived and is thought to be one of the most talented men of all time.

Wow, I've seen a picture of the Mona Lisa.

There are many more famous people that were dyslexics. It is the gift of their dyslexia that made them so brilliant. Just like you, all of these people had the ability to create new information, new designs, new stories, new inventions, etc. Not everyone has this ability.

Don't be discouraged by school. Do your best and ask for help when you need it but remember that just like these other famous dyslexics, you have been given special gifts. Your job in life is to discover what those gifts are and share them with the world.

FAMOUS PEOPLE WITH DYSLEXIA

Benjamin Franklin • Agatha Christie

Hans Christian Anderson • John Lennon

Thomas Edison • Leonardo daVinci

George Washington • Albert Einstein

Alexander Graham Bell • Harry Belafonte

Tom Cruise • Danny Glover • Cher

Whoopi Goldberg • Jay Leno

Henry Ford • Walt Disney • W. B. Yeats

Keanu Reeves • Richard Branson

Kiera Knightley • Edward James Olmos

Oliver Reed • Billy Bob Thornton

Tom Smothers • Robin Williams

Henry Winkler • Loretta Young

Ansel Adams • Ted Turner

Tommy Hilfiger • Pablo Picasso

Robert Rauschenberg • Nolan Ryan

Auguste Rodin • Andy Warhol

Charles Schwab • Magic Johnson

Muhammad Ali • Bruce Jenner

Greg Louganis • F. Scott Fitzgerald

Jackie Stewart • Winston Churchill

Andrew Jackson • Nelson Rockefeller

Gavin Newson • Woodrow Wilson

John F. Kennedy • Thomas Jefferson

Characteristics of Dyslexics

- Intelligent but has problems with reading, writing or spelling

- Often confuses the right from the left

- Intelligent but does not test well or has severe anxiety about testing

- Seems to day dream or zone out when in a classroom or meeting scenario

- Learns best by "hands on" training rather than verbal or written instruction

- Sees movement of letters on a page whether reading or writing

- Reads and rereads without much comprehension

- Has difficulty with spelling

- Has challenges putting thoughts into words

- Difficulty with writing or copying

- Tends to hold a pen or pencil differently and very tightly

- Handwriting is hard to read

- Has difficulty with large or fine motor skills

- Has difficulty reading time on a traditional clock

- Has time management problems

- Tends to be a procrastinator

- Tends to be good at math calculations but word problems are very difficult

- Tends to be disorderly or extremely orderly